GOD IS
Powerful
IN YOU

Discovering and using
your spiritual gifts

*A book of small group agendas
by Paul R. Ford*
with Boyd Pelley

Cell Group Resources
P.O. Box 7847
Houston, Texas 77270 USA
(713) 884-8893 • Fax (713) 742-5998

Copyright © 2008 by Paul R. Ford

All rights reserved. No part of this publication may be
reproduced, sorted in a retrieval system, or transmitted,
in any form by any means, electronic, mechanical,
photocopying, recording or otherwise, without the prior
written permission of the publisher. Printed in the
United States of America.

Cover design by Don Bleyl
Edited by Randall Neighbour

International Standard Book Number: 0-97887799-3-4

All scripture quotations, unless otherwise indicated,
are from the Holy Bible, New International Version,
Copyright © 1973, 1978, 1984 by International Bible Society.
Used by permission.

> *Do not make illegal copies of this book. But you may ...*
> make as many copies as needed from the appendices of this resource, which are designed for duplication. Making copies of any other pages violates copyright laws and is considered theft. Call 800-735-5865 to buy this agenda book in quantity at a substantial savings off the retail price.

Cell Group Resources is a book-publishing division
of TOUCH Outreach Ministries, Inc., a resource,
training, and consulting ministry for churches with
a vision for holistic small groups.

Find us on the web at: www.touchusa.org

Table of Contents

Introduction 5

How to Use This Book 7

Week One: Empowered By Grace 9

Week Two: Discover Your Gifts 17

Week Three: The "I" In Spiritual Gifts 23

Week Four: The "We" In Spiritual Gifts 33

Week Five: The Stewardship Nerve 41

Week Six: Where God Dwells 49

Appendices 57

Introduction

For twenty years I have been mobilizing Christians to use their spiritual gifts, watching the Holy Spirit thrust thousands of believers into life-changing ministry. But a funny thing happened on the way to releasing the Body of Christ to be the body, where each player to uses his or her own God-designed spiritual gifts! God gave me a fresh, innovative way to talk about these amazing grace gifts.

I have the privilege of training Christians in four regions of the world. One area of my work is in Central Asia, formerly the southern part of the Soviet Union. While talking about spiritual gifts in Kazakhstan, I suddenly discovered that the Kazaks have 20 words for sheep but not one word for the concept of "supernatural." Unbelievable!

I had to figure out a way – and quickly – to explain the nature of spiritual gifts to the Kazaks without using my normal words. Here is the idea that came to me: "Spiritual gifts are where God is powerful in you!" While saying these words, I moved my arms in an upward and forward motion, beginning from my stomach and moving out from my chest. That is, spiritual gifts are when God's power rises up within you and moves dynamically outward! When the Spirit of God knows we will not figure out important biblical concepts on our own, he brings them to mind in dramatic yet simple ways. That is what happened to me halfway around the world from my home that day, even as I was powerfully using my own gifts!

This concept has truly revolutionized the way that I talk about spiritual gifts. It is not where you are good at something or comfortable, but rather where you are powerful in the Spirit. It is not your natural skills or strength. It is the dynamic power of God at work, first inside and then outward from you to others.

Let's take a deeper look at this new notion of God's power working in us through our spiritual gifts.

- Paul R. Ford

Paul and I first met in the early 1990s while he was still working on his doctorate from Fuller Seminary. We were both discipleship pastors at local churches and hit it off from our first lunch together. His ideas have so influenced me that I've actually claimed them as my own. One day, I was sharing with him a new, revolutionary idea I had... only to realize I had heard it from him! We had a great laugh together. Such is the nature of friendships and mentoring.

Through the years, the Lord has extended Paul's sphere of influence across the globe, but we've maintained our friendship. I've continued interacting with his latest learnings all along the way. In my ministry on church staff for over 18 years and even in the development of Churchteams, I've sought to live out the principles of equipping and releasing people. In fact, these were the ideas that fueled the earliest vision of developing a web-based tool to enhance disciple making and team building, which is now Churchteams.

One evening after a small group conference, Randall Neighbour and I were enjoying a meal and talking about what was up with TOUCH Publications. He mentioned a writing project that he needed someone to come alongside to work with the author. He didn't even know of Paul's influence in my life! I was amazed at how God orchestrated such a conversation. I wrote curriculum for years because of my role on church staff. Since I felt like I could almost finish Paul's sentences, this was a great fit for me.

I loved working with Paul on this project. It has been a great privilege to call him my friend and to find occasional places that I can come alongside to use my gifts to serve him and by God's grace the Kingdom. It's wonderful to find where you are powerful through Christ. I pray these agendas will help you and your group find God's power through you as well.

- Boyd Pelley

How to Use This Book

Devotionals
Each agenda begins with a personal devotional for you, the small group leader. The best way to use this devotional is to meditate on it each day between your meetings. For example, if your group meets on Thursday evenings, use the next week's devotional to begin your daily devotional time with God on Friday morning, meditating on the scripture each day until the next Thursday. Ask God how the truths discovered in the scripture and devotional should shape how you facilitate the meeting and work with your group members one-on-one.

This Week
The devotional is followed by a brief overview of the agenda, goals for the meeting, and instructions. Reading this insures your small group will understand the point of the agenda and you'll be prepared.

Agendas
The agendas are organized around four W's, which are *Welcome, Worship, Word,* and *Witness*. These four areas are designed to help your group experience Christ's presence, embrace His power, and understand His purposes for your lives to the point of practical application.
- Welcome: An opening question to get your group members involved in the weekly meeting.
- Worship: Practical ways for your group to enter into Christ's presence.
- Word: Applying God's Word to your everyday lives that results in member-to-member ministry in and out of your meetings.
- Witness: "Putting feet" on what you've discussed so your group can live out Christ's purposes for your lives.

In some agendas in this series, you'll notice the order is not as it appears above. This has been done to keep it interesting for your group and set an important tone.

Leader's Notes and Tip Boxes
We've included helpful tip boxes and author's notes under many of the discussion questions to help you understand their meaning. Read through the agenda a few times in the days before your meeting to grasp the direction and outcome of each agenda. Use the notes and tips to prepare, but don't read them aloud during your meeting. They have been placed within the agenda to help you become a better facilitator.

Questions in the Word section
Each numbered question in this section of the agenda has been written so you can simply read it to your group. To increase involvement, write the questions on individual slips of paper and distribute them to various members of your group to read aloud in smaller groups. If you feel these questions should be rephrased to better fit your group or make the meeting more powerful, go for it!

Unless otherwise instructed, keep the last questions in each agenda for yourself as the main facilitator. These are ministry questions that usually require follow up.

Between-the-Meetings Options
Because healthy small group life is more than a once-a-week meeting, it will be important for you to look over these ideas, possibly share them with your group, and then determine which option or options will help your group grow.

If you find implementation to be especially challenging, remember these practical things are what make small group life so powerful and different from other kinds of groups you may have led before. Work as hard at your between-the-meetings activities as you do preparing for your weekly meeting and you'll see growth in yourself and your group.

Scripture Memory Verses
Each agenda ends with a scripture verse, which we highly recommend your group members memorize. There's nothing like scripture memory to keep your mind on glorifying God! Feel free to copy this verse and pass it out to each member as they walk out the door after each meeting. To make it fun, offer a small prize (a candy bar, etc.) for the first person who can recite the verse to you when you next gather for your regular meeting. When you celebrate scripture memory, everyone will join in.

At the back of this book you'll find an appendix with each week's scripture verse on a time-saving, easy-to-duplicate page. This is one area of small group life that you can easily delegate. Ask a member to duplicate the scripture verses and distribute them for you for the next six weeks as the meetings conclude.

Week 1: Empowered by Grace

Your Devotional

> *So when they met together, they asked him, "Lord, are you at this time going to restore the kingdom to Israel?" He said to them: "It is not for you to know the times or dates the Father has set by his own authority. But you will receive power when the Holy Spirit comes on you; and you will be my witnesses in Jerusalem, and in all Judea and Samaria, and to the ends of the earth."* (Acts 1:6-8)

How do you think the disciples felt at this point in the gospel story? What would prompt such a question? They had lived with and learned from Jesus. They watched Him die. They saw Him risen like he said. But they were Jews living under Roman oppression. They knew about kingdoms and power. They were expecting a messiah to come with power to restore Israel's dignity.

God's plan was not for Jesus to become a politician to reinstitute the kingdom of Israel. After all, kingdoms come and go. Nor was His plan to provide contentment and personal comfort. Economies rise and fall. God's plan was for people of every type and time to know Jesus. Oppression, comfort and many other things present obstacles. God knows this and has a plan to get it done. His plan still involves power. But it's power of a different kind. It's the power of God's grace through the Holy Spirit taking on skin.

How about you? Concerning politics and power, do you tend to be indifferent, interested or involved? What about grace and power? Be honest. Which of those three responses best describes you? Why? What would life be like if you became the Holy Spirit's conduit for grace?

As you take your group on a new journey to discover your spiritual gifts, you will certainly find a completely new paradigm for ministry just like the disciples. To prepare your own heart and mind for what you'll experience over the course of the next six weeks, invite God to work through you powerfully in whatever way he chooses. Set your preconceived notions and expectations aside with any desire to be comfortable.

Week 1: Empowered by Grace

This Week

The Objective
This agenda is designed to help members of your group:
1. Understand the Biblical background for spiritual gifts as power that comes from the grace they received at salvation.
2. Increase their curiosity about how God has empowered them.

The Point
Spiritual gifts are not just natural talents or abilities. Spiritual gifts are God's saving grace working itself out in your life in a supernaturally empowered way.

This makes a huge difference in how you develop and use who God has already made you to be. For some, this will mean moving out of your "comfort" zone into the Holy Spirit's "power" zone. For others, this will lead to a new excitement knowing that God has prepared you to minister powerfully by the Holy Spirit.

Preparation
1. Ask your worship leader to find a CD, DVD, or provide the words to "Shout to the Lord" for your time of worship this week.
2. Make copies of Appendix A: Ministry Time Questions (found following week 6). You'll need one set of questions per person. Be sure to leave the back blank for prayer requests.
3. Make copies of Appendix B for each member of your group (each member should have one copy of page 1 and three copies of page 2). If your copier has a magnification feature, increasing the size of these pages will ease completion and give people more room to comment.
3. Go over the between-the-meeting options and collect necessary materials based on the recommendations you are going to make.
4. If your meeting starts late or you anticipate the agenda might be too long, skip the section of questions on Philippians 2:12-13.

Week 1: Empowered by Grace

The Agenda

Welcome
Icebreaker Questions: (Go around the room twice)

1. What is the most powerful gift you ever received? What makes it powerful?

2. In one or two sentences, what have you heard about spiritual gifts?

Worship
Sing "Shout To The Lord" or some other song that has power or majesty as a theme. Use a CD, DVD, or invite someone to accompany with a guitar. When you are finished singing, encourage members to spontaneously speak out phrases as prayers to God describing His power. Close in prayer.

Before you conclude worship this week, the worship leader should ask the group this question:

How do you know when you have really worshipped God? Describe what that's like.

> The point here is to think through together the nature of God's power as we all see it in worship. There's an internal sense of community with God and each other that stirs the emotions as well as the mind to know that we have been in God's presence.

Word
Ask someone to read Ephesians 2:8-10:

> *For it is by grace you have been saved, through faith—and this not from yourselves, it is the gift of God— not by works, so that no one can boast. For we are God's workmanship, created in Christ Jesus to do good works, which God prepared in advance for us to do.*

Week 1: Empowered by Grace

1. Salvation (a right relationship with God) comes by grace as a gift from God we simply receive by faith. What were the sticking points for you to understand and then receive grace?

   > This is a great opportunity to hear someone's testimony about coming to Christ or to share yours. Be as specific as possible in sharing the challenges you faced in coming to Christ. This will help people identify with you. Don't be long-winded, however, you'll lose everyone.

2. We work to earn wages, not gifts. Yet, the last part of this passage talks about us being created to do good works. How do the two work together?

   > Works are the result, outpouring or overflow of grace. Grace empowers the works or purpose for which God created us.

Ask someone to read Philippians 2:12-13:

> *Therefore, my dear friends, as you have always obeyed—not only in my presence, but now much more in my absence—continue to work out your salvation with fear and trembling, for it is God who works in you to will and to act according to his good purpose.*

3. If works are an expression of grace, what does "work out your salvation" mean?

   > **Tip**
   > *Many of the discussion questions this week don't require multiple answers. If the members agree with the first answer, move on to the next question. Focus your time on the ministry questions.*

   > It means to "put skin on God's grace" in one's life (not earn one's salvation through works). This passage challenges us to learn about and master the use of the grace gifts God has given us in the midst of a biblical community.

4. What does "fear and trembling" imply?

   > Power. A sense of authority and accountability, not wanting to do anything to offend God. Another interpretive phrase is "awe and reverence." The bottom line is that there's no reason for a Christian to work out his salvation with others if he has little desire to please his Creator.

Week 1: Empowered by Grace

5. Have you ever had a sense of fear and trembling in using the gifts God has given you? If so, what was that like?

6. From the verse, who is working in you? Why? What difference does it make to know God is orchestrating all this?

Now, let's look at how Paul saw this working in his own life. (Read Ephesians 3:7,8 to your group):

> *I became a servant of this gospel by the gift of God's grace given me through the working of his power. Although I am less than the least of all God's people, this grace was given me: to preach to the Gentiles the unsearchable riches of Christ.*

7. Look over this passage closely, what were the results of God's power in Paul's life?

   He was given grace. He became a servant of the gospel. He was sent to preach to the Gentiles.

8. How have you seen God work powerfully in the lives of others in this group or elsewhere?

9. What do you think the "working of God's power" feels like?

Your Ministry Time

Consider discussing these in triads so that everyone gets a chance to talk them through. Pass out copies of the questions below, found in Appendix A.

10. How does this idea of God's power at work in your life differ from what you've heard or thought about spiritual gifts in the past? How does it make you feel to know God wants to work powerfully through you?

Week 1: Empowered by Grace

11. Paul struggled to use his spiritual gifts. It's not easy to be available to be used by God powerfully. What are you struggling with that keeps you from being used by God more powerfully?

12. Spend a few minutes praying for each other. Ask for permission to lay your hands on the person's shoulder while you are praying. Share and pray for any personal needs as well. (i.e. not prayer requests for friends, relatives, co-workers, etc.)

Witness
1. If God is powerful through us, He wants to extend His grace through us to our friends and family members who don't yet know Christ. Share with the group one or two people that you would like to be a conduit of God's grace.

2. Share one thing from the scripture or our discussion that you found valuable.

> Be sure to let people have time to think through their responses. A couple of minutes of silence and reflection is okay. It is fine to allow members to pass if nothing comes to mind. This may be a whole new way to think about being used by God.

Distribute the copies from Appendix B to each member of your group. Ask everyone to write their name at the bottom of page 59 on all three sheets and give them to three different members in your group to complete and bring to the meeting next week.

Between-the-Meetings Options
The essence of discipleship is learning by doing. Read these options aloud to your members and let the group choose two.

Option #1
Pick a word or phrase from this week's scripture verse. Ask a friend who

Week 1: Empowered by Grace

doesn't know Christ how they would interpret it. (Tell the person it's a homework assignment if doing this makes you feel uncomfortable.)

Option #2
Copy "Appendix C: Gift Card" onto card stock. Hand out these cards and ask everyone to display them in a prominent place like a bathroom mirror or car dashboard. Pray over these gifts each day as a way to become familiar with them for the next few weeks. Then select the 3 to 5 gifts that you think you might have.

Option #3
Decide to use Appendix D: *Listening to God Day by Day* or use your regular journal to record thoughts and prayers each day this week using one of the passages of scripture used in this study.

Option #4
Watch a news program this week. Come to the group next week prepared to share a story of a powerful newsmaker of the week and what made that story powerful.

Option #5
For more insight into the implications of God's power at work in your life, read chapter one of "Knocking Over The Leadership Ladder" by Paul Ford. (Available through touchusa.org or churchsmart.com.)

Option #6
Invest time in personal Bible Study this week looking at these passages of scripture: Exodus 9:10-16, Judges 3:9-11, 6:12-16, Numbers 11:25-26, Psalm 68:28, Ephesians 4:1-8, Colossians 1:24-28. Note your thoughts about God's power at work through people in each of these passages and share it with the group next week.

Scripture for the Week

For it is by grace you have been saved, through faith—and this not from yourselves, it is the gift of God— not by works, so that no one can boast. For we are God's workmanship, created in Christ Jesus to do good works, which God prepared in advance for us to do. (Ephesians 2:8-10)

Week 1: Empowered by Grace

Leader's Weekly Journal

This week, I learned the following about how grace works in a person's life after they become a Christan...

List the qualities of each person in your group that might indicate what his or her spiritual gifts are...

Week 2: Discover Your Gifts

Your Devotional

Then he said to me, "Prophesy to these bones and say to them, 'Dry bones, hear the word of the LORD! This is what the Sovereign LORD says to these bones: I will make breath enter you, and you will come to life. I will attach tendons to you and make flesh come upon you and cover you with skin; I will put breath in you, and you will come to life. Then you will know that I am the LORD.' " (Ezekiel 37:4-6)

The story behind this passage is God revealing His desire to raise up His people. He uses a valley of dry bones to illustrate the deadness of God's people in Ezekiel's day. Surely, this is a picture of many Christians today as well. It may even be true of you. How is your walk with God these days? Is it like a valley of dry bones? What about your group members? If so, there is hope!

In verse 7 of this same passage, something happens when Ezekiel prophesied over the bones as he was commanded to do. God put His breath in these dry bones and brought them to life. Interestingly, the Hebrew word for "breath" is the same word used for the Holy Spirit. God's "breath" is His Spirit filling dry bones with the very fullness of life! God is filling these bones with Himself – His breath – through His Holy Spirit.

In the Old Testament, God would cause His Spirit to come upon people or groups, but then would take the power back. When Jesus ascended into Heaven in Acts 1, the power of the Holy Spirit came to reside in every believer as Jesus promised. The power and vitality of God is available inside each of us in the Body of Christ. Christians are coming to life in a whole new way!

Look inside your heart. Ask the Lord to reveal any T.R.A.P. (Thought, Relationship, Activity, or Possession) that you've not surrendered to Him yet. These are the way of dry bones. Let go and experience the breath of God anew. Then, pray for the dry bones of your group. Ask God to come in power this week and pour out His Holy Spirit on you as you learn more about spiritual gifts.

Week 2: Discover Your Gifts

This Week

The Objective
This agenda is designed to help members of your group:
1. Experience the breath of the Holy Spirit in community as they encourage and build up each other.
2. Discover their spiritual gifts through feedback from others.

The Point
The purpose of spiritual gifts is to build up the body of Christ. Therefore, one of the best ways to discover them is to ask others.

Group members will receive and summarize insights from other group members that will help them discover their spiritual gifts. By sharing insights with others they will become more aware of the gifts and how they work. This interaction will take the depth of your group to a new level of sharing.

Preparation
1. Call each member of your group and encourage them to complete the *What do you think of me?* pages given to them (Appendix B2).
2. Make two copies of Appendix E: *Worship Reading*. Ask two members ahead of time to lead your worship this week and explain to them how it will work. When they arrive at the meeting, give them a copy.
3. Make extra copies of Appendix B1 and 3-5 copies of Appendix B2 for members of your group who were not present last week.
4. Ask your spouse or another person from your group to give you their feedback on your spiritual gifts (use Appendix B2) so that you will be familiar with how the process works.
5. Make copies of Appendix D: *Listening to God Day by Day* (found following week 6). These are a journaling option for your members to use between meetings.
6. Pray for each person in the group by name. Think of who they are and ask God to make clear to them (and to you) how He has made them *powerful*. Pray that they would be willing to use these gifts for ministry outside their "comfort" zones.

Week 2: Discover Your Gifts

The Agenda

Welcome
Icebreaker Questions: (Go around the room twice)

1. What is your most prized possession? Why?

2. What part of your personality, abilities, appearance, or character do you like the best?

Worship
Ask the first person to read Deuteronomy 8:17,18:

> You may say to yourself, "My power and the strength of my hands have produced this wealth for me." But remember the LORD your God, for it is he who gives you the ability ...

Then ask the second person to read 1 Chronicles 29:11-13:

> Yours, O LORD, is the greatness and the power and the glory and the majesty and the splendor, for everything in heaven and earth is yours.
>
> Yours, O LORD, is the kingdom; you are exalted as head over all. Wealth and honor come from you; you are the ruler of all things.
>
> In your hands are strength and power to exalt and give strength to all. Now, our God, we give you thanks, and praise your glorious name.

> When the second person is done reading, instruct the group to be silent for 30 seconds to ponder what they just heard. Encourage the group to focus on a key word or phrase. Then, have the same people read the verses again followed by 30 seconds of silent reflection. Then repeat the process a third time. This will let the content sink in and give members time to process and respond.

Close your worship time with either a prayer of your own or a worship chorus.

Week 2: Discover Your Gifts

Word

Ask everyone to briefly share what they wrote down on each of the pages they were given to complete. As they finish, ask them to hand the page to the person they described.

When everyone has shared and has received their feedback pages, ask them to transfer the summaries from page 59 onto page 58 of Appendix B and tabulate the results.

> **Note About Time Use:**
> *For everyone to receive input during the meeting, each member must be brief and to the point when they share. (Feel free to read this note aloud to the group before you begin to emphasize the need for brevity!)*

Now, ask each person to share their top spiritual gift(s) and then give other members of the group the opportunity to affirm them by sharing something like:

> "I have seen that gift in you ..." or
> "I'm not sure that's where you are MOST powerful because ..."

Watch the time closely on this exercise. It will be easy to go too long. Remember, the goal here is to simply affirm one another to encourage the spiritual gifts discovery process.

Witness

1. Last week, we shared the names of one or two people for whom we would like to be a conduit of God's grace. This week, pair up with one other person from the group and pray for these people.

   Call your members back together after six minutes, and tell them in advance there's only time to pray for their friends, not talk in-depth about prayer requests.

2. As you reflect on share "one thing" from the worship time or from the gifts discovery time that was valuable to them.

   Just as you did last week, give your members a minute to ponder the question and then share. Nothing is wrong with contemplative silence, so don't fill the thinking time with your words.

Discuss the results of last week's "between-the-meeting" assignments.

Week 2: Discover Your Gifts

Between-the-Meetings Options

Option #1
Pray daily for one of the people to whom you gave input concerning their spiritual gifts. Ask the Lord to clearly show them where they are powerfully used by God.

Option #2
Use Appendix D: *Listening to God Day by Day* or your regular journal to record thoughts and prayers each day this week using one of the passages of scripture used in this study.

Option #3
Review your top spiritual gifts and the definitions in Appendix B1. Journal ways you see these in action in your life. Then, look for any obstacles to these gifts being as powerful as God might want them to be.

Option #4
Spend some time in personal Bible Study studying the list of spiritual gifts in Romans 12 and 1 Corinthians 12. These are not exhaustive lists, but they do help you learn more about your gifts. Check cross-references and even search for key words at biblegateway.com or your favorite Bible software.

Option #5
Send an email to everyone in the group so they can "reply all" to everyone else. The leader starts the email, sharing ideas on gifts they think someone else might have. Everyone gets to read all the emails, but each email is directed to one person. When that person receives the email, they must "reply all" and share with one *other* person what gift they think they might have and why. This continues until every person has received and sent a "gift affirmation" email.

Scripture for the Week

> "The Spirit of the Lord came upon him, so that he became Israel's judge and went to war." (Judges 3:10)

Week 2: Discover Your Gifts

Leader's Weekly Journal

Think about the gifts your group sees in you and write them in the space provided below.

On a scale of 1 to 10, how do you feel about possessing each gift?

Think about your meeting. How well did group members interact? What does this say about their relationships with each other?

Write out a prayer asking the Lord to build the relationships within your group. Mention specific relationships by name if those come to mind.

Week 3: The "I" In Spiritual Gifts

Your Devotional

Therefore, I urge you, brothers, in view of God's mercy, to offer your bodies as living sacrifices, holy and pleasing to God—this is your spiritual act of worship. Do not conform any longer to the pattern of this world, but be transformed by the renewing of your mind. Then you will be able to test and approve what God's will is—his good, pleasing and perfect will.

For by the grace given me I say to every one of you: Do not think of yourself more highly than you ought, but rather think of yourself with sober judgment, in accordance with the measure of faith God has given you. (Romans 12:1-3)

Wouldn't it be great to know God's will for your life? It takes a new way of thinking. It is different than the typical way people look at things. The Bible calls it "a renewed mind." But how do you get a renewed mind?

Verse 3 shows you how. Start by dealing with your pride. Stop thinking of yourself like the world revolves around you. Instead, get real about yourself (what the Apostle Paul called sober judgment). Go to the One who designed you and see what He had in mind.

I (Paul) highly respect a godly man named Tim. I used to admire him so much I wanted to be exactly like him. I thought that if I could just speak like Tim and relate to people like Tim, then I would be most useful to God. I wanted to be more than I really am. Then, through a series of events I discovered that I made a horrible Tim! Slowly but surely, I realized that I was designed to be a powerful Paul with my own unique part to play.

How about you? Do you struggle with thinking too much of yourself? Or maybe you think too little of yourself. Both are rooted in pride because both are focused on you! Instead, live by faith out of the grace you have been given. What does God enjoy about how He made you? Think about that awhile. When you find answers to this question, you will be well down the path to knowing God's will for your life.

Week 3: The "I" In Spiritual Gifts

This Week

The Objective
This agenda is designed to help members of your group:
1. Understand that knowing God's will begins with discovering who He has designed them to be.
2. Develop a "sober estimation" of who they are according to their spiritual gifts.
3. Reflect on their ministry activities and whether they are aligned with God's design for them.

The Point
Knowing God's will begins with knowing your spiritual gifts. It just makes sense that God would have designed you for the purposes He has for you. Knowing your spiritual gifts requires intentional time and focus.

As you mature in your faith, you will more clearly understand your spiritual gifts. It is important to have a balanced, realistic view of yourself - not to think too highly or too lowly of yourself. This is called have a "sober estimation" of who you are. The better you understand your gifts, the more power you will see God working through you in your ministry activities.

Preparation
1. Jot down your thoughts/responses to the questions in the agenda and any follow up questions you might want to ask your group.
2. Ask a member of your group to find a CD of appropriate instrumental worship music and a player to use during the worship time.
3. Make a copy of Appendix F ("Week 3 - *Welcome & Ministry Questions*") for each member of the group.
4. Pray for each person in the group by name.
5. Contact each member and ask them to bring the spiritual gifts pages given to them last week and their Bible when they come to the meeting.

Week 3: The "I" In Spiritual Gifts

The Agenda

Welcome

Tell your group the following: "Let's begin by practicing the process of sober estimation. What is sober estimation? We'll get there! But first, let's break into pairs and answer the following questions. You have just 2 minutes each to share your answers." (Hand out the questions as you share this.)

> **This Week's Icebreaker:**
> *Pass out copies of the first three questions to each person (found in Appendix F). Then, read the last three questions aloud one at a time.*

1. Where did you live between the ages of 6 and 12?

2. What or where was a special place for you to go at that time in your life?

3. Who was one person who was always there when you needed him or her during those years?

Now ask the pairs to turn back to back with his or her partner. Without turning around, ask everyone to answer the following questions:

4. What color are your partner's eyes?

5. What color is your partner's shirt of blouse?

6. Who was someone special to your partner as a child?

Finally, ask everyone to sit down, and ask: How many got all three right? Why did you answer any of these questions incorrectly?

> We miss a lot with casual observation and listening. To really understand someone you have to pay attention and be more intentional. The same is true with understanding who you are in Christ. It is going to take extra thought, prayer, and looking at yourself from different angles.

Week 3: The "I" In Spiritual Gifts

Worship

Instructions for your worship leader:

With quiet instrumental music on CD in the background, read Psalm 139 as a group. Go around the circle of your group and ask each person to read one verse. Keep going around until you are finished with this Psalm. Read it prayerfully to our magnificent God!

When your group has read the chapter, close in prayer.

As a lead in for the Word time, conclude with a prayer of dedication for the meeting:

> **Tip:**
> Turn on the instrumental music before your meeting begins, keeping the volume low. This will set a worship-centered tone for reading through Psalm 139.

"Father as we look more closely at how you uniquely made each one of us, we offer ourselves as living sacrifices, longing to be holy and pleasing to you. Here we are. In Jesus name, Amen."

Word

Ask someone to read Romans 12:1-2:

> *Therefore, I urge you, brothers, in view of God's mercy, to offer your bodies as living sacrifices, holy and pleasing to God—this is your spiritual act of worship. Do not conform any longer to the pattern of this world, but be transformed by the renewing of your mind. Then you will be able to test and approve what God's will is—his good, pleasing and perfect will.* (Romans 12:1-2)

1. Most followers of Christ are concerned about confidently knowing God's will for their lives. Has this been an easy or difficult thing for you? Why?

    In the next verse in Romans 12, Paul provides specific guidance on how to know God's will. It starts by renewing your mind, by changing the way you think.

Week 3: The "I" In Spiritual Gifts

Ask the same person to read the next verse, Romans 12:3:

> *For by the grace given me I say to every one of you: Do not think of yourself more highly than you ought, but rather think of yourself with sober judgment, in accordance with the measure of faith God has given you. (Romans 12:3)*

Now ask your group either 2a or 2b (your choice):

2a. Looking back on your life, was there a time you thought about yourself either too highly or too poorly? What was that time like for you? What helps you have a more sober perspective of yourself?

2b. Without sharing names, how do you recognize someone who thinks more highly of themselves than they ought? How about someone who thinks too little of themselves? What lies underneath both of these extremes?

> In both cases, people tend to look right past you and pay little attention to anything but their own agenda. Pride is at the heart of both these self-perspectives. "It's all about me!" People naturally feel they are more important or better than others.

3. In contrast, Paul tells you to think differently by thinking of yourself with sober judgment. What is sober judgment?

> Sober judgment is a realistic view of yourself in your proper context.

Ask someone to read Timothy 1:11:

> *And of this gospel I was appointed a herald and an apostle and a teacher.*
> *(2 Timothy 1:11)*

4. Here, Paul gives a sober estimate of who he is in Christ. His spiritual gifts give him the ability to understand who he is better. How many gifts does he have? What are they? How do you suppose he figured these out?

Week 3: The "I" In Spiritual Gifts

> Herald (evangelism), apostle, teacher — 3 gifts. Most people have 1-3 primary gifts that blend together. You learn them by input from others, using them, and thinking intentionally about how and where God works powerfully through you.

Read this aloud to your group: "Since spiritual gifts reveal the power and grace of God in our lives, they are not what we do for God, but rather a part of who we are! Paul models this for us in Romans 15:17-20. As Paul talks about his ministry, his identity through his spiritual gifts forcefully rises up through his words."

Read Romans 15:17-20 and ask the following question.

5. Which of Paul's spiritual gifts show up clearly in this passage? Where?

    > Evangelism gift shown clearly — proclaim the gospel, reaching the gospel where Christ was not known. Apostles are dynamic spiritual foundation builders ... see verse 20. Also the reference to signs and wonders in verse 19 for Paul is a validation of his apostolic gifting (see 2 Cor. 12:12).

6. Last week, you had the opportunity to hear from others their perspective of where you are powerful with your spiritual gifts. Now, we want to hear your sober estimation of how God is powerful in you. Pull out your list and definitions. What 2-3 gifts do you feel like best describe God's working through you? Why? (As everyone shares, write down their top gifts in the space below.)

Week 3: The "I" In Spiritual Gifts

7. How might identifying your spiritual gifts give you a clearer picture of God's will for your life? Based on the gifts you sense God has given you, what types of activities would energize you?
What types of activities would drain you?

Your Ministry Time

Break up into triads to answer these next two questions and pray (distribute Appendix F).

8. How aligned are your ministry/service/volunteer commitments with your spiritual gifts? Is there something you are not doing that you should be? Is there something you are doing you shouldn't be?

The 65-35 Rule:
"What if I'm involved in a ministry that doesn't suit my gifts?"

One cannot sustain ministry for a long period of time in areas in which he or she is not gifted. That's why so many people burn out. Adjust your ministry activities so you are spending 65% of the time in your "sweet spot." In any family, there are chores to do, but try to keep the chores to less than 35% of your ministry effort. You will find this a sustainable ministry pace.

9. How might the amount of faith you currently possess influence your ability to have a "sober estimate" of yourself?

Take time now to pray aloud in your triad for yourself in the area of sober judgment, asking God to reveal his power and grace in your life. Be sure to pray in first person and "own" your prayers tonight.

Witness
Ask your group to get in the same pairs as last week when they prayed for their unchurched friends. Invite them to dialog about ways they should use their spiritual gift to bless one of these friends this week.

Call the group back together, standing in a circle holding hands. Go around the circle, asking each person to share "one thing" from scripture or the discussion that was valuable to them.

Week 3: The "I" In Spiritual Gifts

Between-the-Meetings Options
The activities your group does between the meetings are what make the material in this agenda book "stick." This week, emphasize the importance of following through on the options your members choose. Remind them that you want this series to be life changing!

Encourage your group to choose option #1 plus one other option.

Option #1
Call an unchurched friend and tell them you need their help with an assignment given to you by your small group leader. Explain that you've just learned what your spiritual gifts are (sharing your top three), and ask the person which ones are most evident. (Honest feedback from respected unchurched friends is the assignment.)

Option #2
Read chapters two and three of "Knocking Over The Leadership Ladder" by Paul Ford.

Option #3
Ask your spouse or a close friend who knows you well if (and when) there are times you come across either as arrogant or self-depreciating.

Option#4
Over dinner with a friend, your spouse, or your family, share a time you know you came across as arrogant. Then, invite them to do the same. After everyone has had the opportunity to share, talk about the good quality within each one of you that went bad, causing the appearance of arrogance.

Option #5
If arrogance is a problem for you, pick one day this week to fast from either one or all meals that day. Use the extra time for prayer, asking the Lord to reveal the root of the arrogance and confess it as sin. Then, petition God for what he has for you to meet that need as a replacement.

Week 3: The "I" In Spiritual Gifts

Option #6
While you are driving this week, identify ways that your driving indicates a poor sober-estimation of yourself. Be ready to share your insights with the group next week. (If you have difficulty with this exercise, invite your spouse or a child to help you see where you need help!)

Scripture for the Week

> *"But you will receive power when the Holy Spirit has come upon you; and you will be my witnesses in Jerusalem, and in all Judea and Samaria, and to the ends of the earth."* (Acts 1:8)

Week 3: The "I" In Spiritual Gifts

Leader's Weekly Journal
What impact does the answer to question #8 in this week's agenda have on your current roles in ministry?

Finish this sentence:
I think too little or too much of myself in the areas of...

Week 4: The "We" In Spiritual Gifts

Your Devotional

Love must be sincere. Hate what is evil; cling to what is good. Be devoted to one another in brotherly love. Honor one another above yourselves. Never be lacking in zeal, but keep your spiritual fervor, serving the Lord. Be joyful in hope, patient in affliction, faithful in prayer. Share with God's people who are in need. Practice hospitality. (Romans 12:9-13)

Have you ever been in a ministry setting where the tension was so thick you could cut it with a knife? What's that about? Aren't we all supposed to just get along? The problem in such settings is that the "I" gets in the way of the "We" and the result is *conflict*.

Americans are uniquely focused on "I" rather than "We" for a number of reasons. A Russian observer of an American mission team said it best: "Why doesn't your team go home until the team members like each other, and *then* come back to share the Gospel effectively as a team?" When these same team members understood and appreciated each other's ministry identity, it helped them choose the way of love.

Romans 12 is one of the key passages on spiritual gifts. It is no coincidence that the verses above immediately follow Paul's discussion on gifts. Another major passage on spiritual gifts, 1 Corinthians 12, is followed by the love chapter, 1 Corinthians 13. Love harnesses the power of grace (and spiritual gifts) by bringing control and unity.

There is a lot of power when people use their spiritual gifts *together*. This will create disunity unless that power is harnessed by love. Sincere love has a way of bringing control and unity. Embracing Christ's sacrificial love is vital to working together!

This week, examine your heart. Is there some area of your life that lacks control or a relationship that lacks unity? How could you introduce love and grace into that situation or relationship?

Look at the directives in the verses above: Love, hate, cling, be devoted, honor, never be lacking, keep, serve, be joyful, patient, faithful, share, and practice. That's a boat load of amazing attributes. Which one brings conviction for you today?

Week 4: The "We" In Spiritual Gifts

This Week

The Objective
This agenda is designed to help members of your group:
1. Understand that spiritual gifts have no meaning outside of body life.
2. Consider how well they are contributing to the life of your small group and your church.
3. Discover how to work well together.

The Point
Deep in every one of us is the desire to belong. We were made to live in community with other people. However, belonging means more than just attending a function with people. It also means being involved.

Spiritual gifts were given to people to exercise in their small group, church and the world. They have little use outside of these contexts or as individuals working alone. The "I" in spiritual gifts finds it's greatest power in the context of "We!"

Preparation
1. Talk with your worship leader to select a chorus or song that fits the topic of worshipping together or community.
2. Make copies of "Appendix G: Week 4 - *Dream*" to hand out during the Word time.
3. Prepare your response to question 6 (same as "Appendix G: Dream) ahead of time to give as an example for the group to follow. This will help you know how to instruct your group to write out a response of their own.

Week 4: The "We" In Spiritual Gifts

The Agenda

Welcome
Icebreaker Question:

In working with teams or a group of people, what was the worst and best experiences you ever had? Why?

> **Tip:**
> *Write out the icebreaker on a slip of paper and give it to the newest member of your group to share tonight. Leading the icebreaker time is great on-the-job training for future leaders!*

Worship
Ask your worship leader to begin your worship time by praying for each other. Have each one who wants to participate complete this sentence:

"Father, thank you for _____, in him/her I see _____."

Make sure every person present is mentioned and recognized.

Now, sing 2-3 worship songs focusing on worshipping together (ie, "Bind us together" or, "We are one in the bonds of love") and close in prayer.

Word
Read the following paragraph to your group:

"Last week we looked at making a sober estimation of ourselves so that we can best invest our spiritual gifts. This week, we continue in Romans 12 to better understand the environment in which these gifts are designed to work."

Now ask someone to read Romans 12:4,5:

> *Just as each of us has one body with many members, and these members do not all have the same function, so in Christ we who are many form one body, and each member belongs to all the others.* (Romans 12:4,5)

Week 4: The "We" In Spiritual Gifts

1. Has anyone experienced a sickness or injury that disabled you? What happened?

2. What is the point of Paul's metaphor of the body in these verses?

3. How does it make you feel to know that you belong?

   > God's context for your growth is to see yourself clearly as a player in the body of Christ. There is no one more important! Everyone has a part and every part is essential. You belong.

4. Let's review. Where do gifts come from?

   > Grace. In the Greek it says, "according to God's charis (grace), each of us has different charismata (gifts). So many people are looking for their place in life, where they can fit in and make a difference. For the Christian, that begins with understanding how God has "graced" us!

   > **Note:**
   > *Less than one in ten believers have stopped to seriously examine who they are in Christ! Most people simply do not know how to do this, or what to examine. Challenge your members to focus tonight and in the days to follow to let this week's content sink in and do a deep work in their minds and hearts!*

5. Paul says that we are to use our spiritual gifts to their *full potential*. What would it look like if you were to use your spiritual gifts to their full potential? Write down your answer to this question on the supplied worksheet and read your response to the group.

   > Distribute the copies of "Appendix G: Week 4 - Dream" to each person in your group. Give your members 5-10 minutes to complete the worksheet.

6. Ask your members to complete this sentence: "If I were using my spiritual gifts to their full potential..."

   > Spiritual gifts—being used well—always benefit the body of Christ. Spiritual gifts only make sense in the context of community. This is the "we" in spiritual gifts.

Week 4: The "We" In Spiritual Gifts

7. What happens to a small group if people are not using their spiritual gifts? Or, if only one or two people are using their gifts?

    Answers should include: burn out; the group "goes nowhere"; participation wanes; poor attendance; or the group becomes spiritually sterile.

8. What happens to a small group if everyone is contributing by using their gifts?

    This is the context for seeing God's power working directly through the group for one another and a hurting world. There is nothing like team or community done right! When each member of a group is contributing by using their gifts, transformation takes place and there is personal and numeric growth in the group.

9. Everyone loves a winning team because they all work hard and work together. On a scale of 1-5, how well do you think you are contributing to this team? (5 being a strong contributor.)

10. What obstacles have you found that keep teams or groups from working well? (Ask everyone to write the shared obstacles on the back of the sheet of paper used earlier.)

    Answers include: Conflict over direction; different levels of ability; poor coaching; unclear goals; don't know what position to play; unsure how to play that position, etc. It is not a coincidence that these verses follow.

Ask someone to read Romans 12:9-13

Love must be sincere. Hate what is evil; cling to what is good. Be devoted to one another in brotherly love. Honor one another above yourselves. Never be lacking in zeal, but keep your spiritual fervor, serving the Lord. Be joyful in hope, patient in affliction, faithful in prayer. Share with God's people who are in need. Practice hospitality. (Romans 12:9-13)

Week 4: The "We" In Spiritual Gifts

11. Re-consider your list of obstacles. How might the directives given in these verses address each of those obstacles?

Your Ministry Time

Break up into two groups tonight. The groups can be mixed or men's and women's groups. (Establish facilitators for both groups beforehand.)

12. Which one of the directives in Romans 12:9-13 are most compelling to you personally? Why?

Now, spend time as a group asking the Lord to bring the qualities listed in Romans 12:9-13 to your group and your church.

> **Tip:**
> *If you choose to break up into men's and women's group tonight, this would be a good opportunity to ask the men and women if they need to confess anything or receive ministry for sensitive issues.*

Witness

Gather your members back together. Ask them to share what they were told this last week when they asked an unbelieving friend for feedback concerning their spiritual gifts.

Finish up your time together by asking each person to share "one thing" from scripture or the discussion that was valuable to them.

Between-the-Meetings Options

Pair group members with a partner and together choose 2 of the options below that they will do. Ask them to check in with the other one at least once to quote this week's scripture verse and share how they are doing with the action step.

Option #1
Take advantage of at least two opportunities to demonstrate love to others by being courteous in a way that you might not be courteous. Examples: Hold the car door for your wife; say "thank you" at a time you might not usually do so; let someone else go first in line, and so on.

Week 4: The "We" In Spiritual Gifts

Option #2
Partner with one other person in your group to talk together about how you can use your gifts to together to love or serve others. Remain creative as you think about how to use your specific mix of gifts to bless others. Report to the group next week on what you're doing together.

Option #3
Secret friend. Put everyone's name on a piece of paper and place it in a container. Have each person randomly select a name of someone else in the group. Their job this week is to make this person feel loved by sending a note, leaving a gift, meeting a need, or any other creative way to express love or appreciation. Couples can help each other or trade names if they want.

Option #4
Plan an event or outing related to your unchurched friends' skills, talents, or interests. Invite a member of the group to join the two of you in that event or outing. (Example: play golf; go shopping; do some wood-working; walk a park; play a sport; go to the movies.)

Scripture for the Week

"For by the grace given me I say to each one of you: Do not think more highly of yourself than you ought, but rather think of yourself with sober judgment, in accordance with the measure of faith God has given you."   *(Romans 12:3)*

Week 4: The "We" In Spiritual Gifts

Leader's Weekly Journal
Reflect on your responses to your "dream ministry." Now that you are done with this session, how has it changed or sharpened? Write out a prayer once again committing your ministry to the Lord.

As you think about your members responses this week and their giftings, which of them seems like they might be a good apprentice and eventual group leader? How might you help them along?

Week 5: The Stewardship Nerve

Your Devotional

Jesus told his disciples: "There was a rich man whose manager was accused of wasting his possessions. So he called him in and asked him, 'What is this I hear about you? Give an account of your management, because you cannot be manager any longer.'"

The manager said to himself, 'What shall I do now? My master is taking away my job. I'm not strong enough to dig, and I'm ashamed to beg— I know what I'll do so that, when I lose my job here, people will welcome me into their houses.'" (Luke 16:1)

Have you ever lost a job or been fired? It is an agonizing circumstance in which to find yourself. Lots of worry, sleepless nights, and family arguments. And, then, there's the questioning. What did I do wrong? How could I have done better?

When you are entrusted a responsibility at work, there is an expectation that you will fulfill that responsibility. Most of the time, you will be given the training you need. After a period of time, you are expected to perform your assigned task. This expectation is monitored to determine how well you do what you are supposed to do. This monitoring process from the perspective of the manager is called *stewardship*. Stewardship, like nerves in the body, keeps you alert to sense the pain of something not going right and the pleasure of things working well. What happened to the manager in this parable when he failed at his duties? (Read verses 3-15). How did he feel when he learned his fate? What action did he take? How were his actions received by his employer?

Stewardship is serious stuff. Jesus knew it and taught that we must be faithful with the little things we're given. Do them well, and greater opportunities to use our gifts will come.

How well are you stewarding the gifts you've been given? If you performed your work like you are using your spiritual gifts, would you still have a job? Would you be up for a promotion, a demotion, or get fired? Ask the giver of your gifts for *his* evaluation and work diligently to use what you've been given to receive more.

Week 5: The Stewardship Nerve

This Week

The Objective
This agenda is designed to help members of your group:
1. Grasp that they are stewards or managers of the gifts God has given them.
2. Look at their spiritual gifts through a broader lens ... powerful in words or powerful in actions.

The Point
Every Christian should have a basic desire to please God. To please God means to do that which He has given. As you gain a clear understanding of your God-given role, there is an expectation that you will live out that responsibility; that you will be a good steward of what God has given you.

Your role in pleasing God and building his kingdom is further clarified by simply discerning whether your particular gifts are more powerful in words or in actions.

Preparation
1. Read and prepare for the meeting through the notes in the Welcome, Word and Witness sections of the study. Jot down your thoughts or responses to the questions and any follow up questions you may ask.
2. Locate enough towels and water basins for half the people in your group and fill them with warm water for the worship time just before the meeting begins. It will be powerful to ask your worship leader or someone else in the group to lead the activity on washing feet.
3. Make enough copies of Appendix H: Week 5 - "Powerful in Words or Actions" for each member of your group. Keep extra pens on hand for the meeting.
4. Find a pocket mirror and keep it handy for use during the meeting.

Week 5: The Stewardship Nerve

The Agenda

Welcome
As a review, look back over your spiritual gifts.
1. What potential spiritual gifts do you have? These are the possible places where God shows up powerfully in who you are. Share with us no more than two or three gifts, not five or six.

   > Making a sober estimate (week 3) means seriously focusing in on the possibilities. We are not looking for the final decision on what your gifts might be. Rather, we are sharing our best understanding of the top 2 to 3 probable gifts, given what we know so far. You are in the process of discovery.

2. How have you seen others in the group using their gifts? Let's use this as a time to listen and affirm gifts as we move into worship!

   > Spiritual gifts are best confirmed by others in the body of Christ who have observed God's power working through you.

Worship
Read this to your group:
"This week, we're going to experience worship by washing each other's feet. It was adopted by Christians as a humble act of service reflecting devotion to Christ. Let's humbly wash each other's feet as devoted followers of Christ for worship tonight."

> Instruct everyone to get into pairs (men with men, women with women) and remove their shoes and socks. Distribute the basins and towels.

Now, instruct the group members to take turns washing the other person's feet while you read John 13:1-9 aloud.

When everyone's feet have been washed—and you've washed someone's feet as well—ask someone close in a prayer.

Week 5: The Stewardship Nerve

Word

Invite someone who doesn't typically volunteer to read 1 Peter 4:10,11:

> *Each one should use whatever gift he has received to serve others, faithfully administering God's grace in its various forms. If anyone speaks, he should do it as one speaking the very words of God. If anyone serves, he should do it with the strength God provides, so that in all things God may be praised through Jesus Christ.* (1 Peter 4:10,11)

1. Body life is a metaphor that Paul uses often in his writing. In the human body, what role do the nerves play?

    Like nerves in a body, there has to be constant communication between the players in the body of Christ and the head who is Christ. This process of communication and accountability is what we call stewardship.

2. If anyone in the group has worked as a cashier or teller, what was your perspective of the money you were entrusted with? How is managing something for someone else different than owning it?

3. Building on this idea, what is significant about the idea that you are to manage (steward) the grace God has given you through your spiritual gifts?

    Being a manager or steward of gifts takes this series from an academic exercise to a practical thing to live out. People may feel anything from excited to coerced to use their gifts.

> **Tip:**
> *Question #4 could be set up as a debate between two teams in your group. Each side would a) present its case, b) offer arguments against the other presentation, and c) rebut the arguments from the other team.*
>
> *If you decide to do this, watch the clock! It could become very time-consuming.*

4. Verse 10 says you are to use your gifts to serve others. So, if the purpose of gifts is serving other people, which is more important, others' needs or your gifts? Why?

Week 5: The Stewardship Nerve

5. What two broad types of gifts does Peter identify in verse 11? Why is this distinction helpful?

Distribute a copy of Appendix H: *Powerful in Words or Actions* to each group member. Ask each member to fill it out.

7. Share your responses to question 3 in Appendix H.

Re-read 1 Peter 4:11.

Ask everyone to paraphrase this verse for themselves and share it with the group.

> **Tip:**
> *Be sure to go first when you do this activity. Look into the pocket mirror and speak to yourself to model this for your group.*

> Example: "Boyd, since your gift is administration, be sure you are working on tasks in ways to serve people rather than expecting them to serve the tasks. That's when you'll be powerful." Speak to yourself, using your own name, to show the group how it should be done. If people balk, tell them you know they talk to themselves in the mirror from time to time, and you're just asking them to do it in front of the group tonight!

Witness

Ask your group members to share one thing from scripture or the discussion that was valuable to them.

1. Do any of you interact with the same unchurched person(s) on a regular basis (ie, at work or school each day)?

2. What difference would it make to bring that person in on your relationship with God and other members of this group? How can we do this in the next month?

> Brainstorm ways to connect with unchurched friends such as parties, game nights, going to a ball game and servanthood opportunities (auto repair; moving furniture; babysitting).

Week 5: The Stewardship Nerve

Between-the-Meetings Options

Option #1
Call two other people in the group and ask them to repeat what they looked in the mirror and said to themselves this week during the meeting. This will help everyone remember where they are powerfully used by God.

Option #2
Plan a weekend evening together. Each person should bring a dish that best illustrates their spiritual gift. Don't share what you're bringing beforehand or with any of the members of the group. Over the meal, guess why each person brought their dish.

Option #3
Read chapter 6 in "Knocking Over the Leadership Ladder" by Paul Ford and write down the best ideas found in the chapter.

Option #4
Write out 25 different ways to steward God's grace. Have lunch with another member in the group doing the same thing and compare notes.

Option #5
Mix up the meeting next week. Look at your spiritual gifts and use them accordingly. If you have the gift of hospitality, open your home for the meeting. If your gift is giving, buy the food for the snacks. If your gift is evangelism, bring an unchurched friend to the meeting. If your gift is helps, show up an hour early to the meeting and offer to help the host tidy up. To make it *really* different, appoint a new, temporarily leader for the group based on their gift of leadership and ask the existing leader to just show up to the meeting.

Scripture for the Week

If anyone speaks he/she should do it as if speaking the very words of God, If anyone serves, he/she should do it with the strength God provides, so that in all things God may be praised through Jesus Christ. To Him be the glory and the power forever and ever. Amen. (1 Peter 4:11)

Week 5: The Stewardship Nerve

Leader's Weekly Journal

Write out your thoughts on what stewardship means in general and what it means for you specifically.

List your group members who are powerful in words. Then, list those powerful in actions. Also, list those that are both. (Use page 48).

Now, write down one idea about how you might help them be a good steward of their gifts in and outside your group.

Week 5: The Stewardship Nerve

Week 6: Where God Dwells

Your Devotional

I pray that out of his glorious riches he may strengthen you with power through his Spirit in your inner being, so that Christ may dwell in your hearts through faith. And I pray that you, being rooted and established in love, may have power, together with all the saints, to grasp how wide and long and high and deep is the love of Christ, and to know this love that surpasses knowledge—that you may be filled to the measure of all the fullness of God.

Now to him who is able to do immeasurably more than all we ask or imagine, according to his power that is at work within us, to him be glory in the church and in Christ Jesus throughout all generations, for ever and ever! Amen. *(Ephesians 3:16-21)*

Have you ever been in a worship service when God showed up? Everyone knew he was there and you could feel his powerful, engaging presence. Maybe you've experienced the same thing in a small group when it seems God is there and everyone is alert and involved in the discussion or ministry time. Maybe you've been part of a ministry team that was working together and you could tell that God was working through your team powerfully.

The apostle Paul loved the Church in Ephesus. They had a special place in his heart. It was natural that this prayer would flow from his heart to God concerning them. He longed to see God's power realized in their midst. He knew it came from love, from community and most of all from passionate devotion to Jesus. He wanted more than anything else for them to know and experience the power of love. He knew if they knew God's love and grace individually, and if they would search for it collectively, then God himself would show up with power to reveal his glory to all people for all time!

What would it be like for God to take over your group this week? What if he took over your heart completely today? What would it be like if God actually did immeasurably more than all you are asking or imagining? Now, that's power at work within us!

Each day this week, petition God for this kind of breakthrough.

Week 6: Where God Dwells

This Week

The Objective
1. Realize that God powerfully dwells in a group of believers willing to share their lives and gifts with each other.
2. Summarize and identify points of application of this study.

The Point
God is building his body, the Church, using each part of the body (you and me) in relationship with each other to become His actual dwelling place. God "hangs out" where his people are in relationship with each other. Here is where his power is most fully known and realized.

Preparation
1. Make copies of "Appendix I: Week 6 - *Powerfully Moving Out in Practical Ways*" for everyone in the group for the Welcome portion of the meeting.
2. Ask your worship leader to select a chorus or song to end the prayer time that fits the topic of unity.
3. Be ready with your response to question 8 so that you have something thoughtful to say to affirm every person in your group.
4. Pray for each person in the group by name. Pray that they would find good application of their gifts for the body and that together your group would experience God's powerful presence.

Week 6: Where God Dwells

The Agenda

Welcome

Start today's gathering by handing out copies of Appendix I: "Powerfully Moving Out in Practical Ways." Give your group members 3-5 minutes to fill out the tool.

Ask each person to share their response to the questions, allowing time for group response.

> After each person shares, ask the rest of the group to share any ways they have seen that person do those things well or any other ideas about how they might practically move out with their spiritual gift.

Worship

In Jesus' last prayer he prayed for unity among believers across cultures and time. Read this prayer and then voice your own prayers of worship and adoration of the God who makes us one. Thank him for the unity He brings. Then, close with a brief chorus on community.

> *"My prayer is not for them alone. I pray also for those who will believe in me through their message, that all of them may be one, Father, just as you are in me and I am in you. May they also be in us so that the world may believe that you have sent me. I have given them the glory that you gave me, that they may be one as we are one: I in them and you in me. May they be brought to complete unity to let the world know that you sent me and have loved them even as you have loved me."*
>
> *"Father, I want those you have given me to be with me where I am, and to see my glory, the glory you have given me because you loved me before the creation of the world. Righteous Father, though the world does not know you, I know you, and they know that you have sent me. I have made you known to them, and will continue to make you known in order that the love you have for me may be in them and that I myself may be in them."* (John 17:20-26)

Week 6: Where God Dwells

Word
Ask someone to read Ephesians 2:19-22:

> *Consequently, you are no longer foreigners and aliens, but fellow citizens with God's people and members of God's household, built on the foundation of the apostles and prophets, with Christ Jesus himself as the chief cornerstone. In him the whole building is joined together and rises to become a holy temple in the Lord. And in him you too are being built together to become a dwelling in which God lives by his Spirit.* (Ephesians 2:19-22)

1. The verses preceding 19-22 talk about the divide between Jews and Gentiles. To the Jews, anyone else was a "foreigner or alien." Have you ever felt out of place because of your race, gender, faith, or conviction? If so, when? What does it feel like to be a foreigner or alien?

2. What difference does being a part of a church make for you and your family?

> In a broader sense, you are part of God's worldwide family. Many missionaries and international Christians have found that there is something powerfully bonding between believers whether or not they even speak the same language. Obviously, this bond is their faith in Christ realized through the Holy Spirit that dwells in each of them.

Ask the person who read the verses from Ephesians to read them again.

3. What spiritual gifts or ministry identity roles are specifically mentioned? What roles do you think the other gifts play in building this household of God?

4. What is a cornerstone? How does this relate to Jesus? What happens if the cornerstone becomes weak or is removed?

Week 6: Where God Dwells

5. In Christ, we are being built together. Why is this so important?

> Each one of us is one building block. Outside of our relationship with others, our spiritual gifts and lives are incomplete and far from reaching their full potential. God is building us together.

6. According to these verses, what is it that God is building?

> Share with the group that the temple was the set aside place where God interacted with his people in the Old Testament. It was known as the place where God dwells. People would come from all over the country and the world to be in this place where God was. It was the place people came for forgiveness, direction, and a sense of community.

7. God's power and His presence are best realized in community because it is where He dwells. What is so compelling about life together with other believers?

> In God's house there is forgiveness, direction, and community. This is extremely attractive to most people. It is also the place where the Spirit of God lives and moves and has His way as we share our body life gifts and build up one another.

8. How have you experienced the presence of God in this small group of friends these past six weeks?

Your Ministry Time

Tonight, take time for group members to edify one another. Invite them to pray aloud with a sentence of thanks for various members of the group. Encourage them to be specific when they pray.

If anyone needs healing, encourage them to speak up and get prayer tonight. Challenge the members of your group to listen to the Holy Spirit before they pray to hear what God wants to say or do through them.

Week 6: Where God Dwells

Witness

1. Finish up your time together by asking each person to share "one thing" from scripture or the discussion that was valuable to them.

2. Give everyone a minute to share their greatest "aha" moments from this series.

3. What should we do with what we've learned?

4. How have interactions with your friends who do not yet know Christ changed since you learned about your spiritual gifts?

Close your time discussing plans for the next topic of discussion and any necessary plans for upcoming meetings, get-togethers or other events.

After-the-Series Options

For a more in-depth consideration of God's power in you, have each person select one of the first three options and decide together whether or not your group should do options #4, 5, or 6.

Option #1
Get together with a friend from the group and review each of the six verses you have memorized. Talk about the series and which of the verses best encapsulates it for you.

Option#2
As you think about your top spiritual gifts, list 2-3 specific ministry areas you are interested in and how your spiritual gifts might be used in your church and your small group. Now pick the top one. Ask the Lord to show you how to more powerfully focus your spiritual gifts for greater ministry impact. Follow through by sharing your insights with your pastor or a ministry leader.

Week 6: Where God Dwells

Option #3
Do a web search on "free personality assessment" and complete it when you find it. Compare the results to your spiritual gifts. Do you see any similarities? How might your personality influence your spiritual gifts?

Option #4
For a more in-depth look at your spiritual gifts and ministry identity, consider going through the assessments and discussion guide entitled *Discovering Your Ministry Identity* by Paul Ford (available at www.churchsmart.com).

Option #5
For a more in-depth look at your baseline personality profile and how it empowers your spiritual gifts, check out *The Grip Birkman Blueprint*. (www.gripbirkmanblueprint.com or www.gbbcoaches.net).

Option #6
Stay connected! Churchteams.com was co-founded by co-author, Boyd Pelley. This web-based software connects people to groups, enhances communication between groups and staff, and helps small group ministries track information and grow. Check it out at www.churchteams.com/touch

Scripture for the Week

> *Each one should use whatever gift he/she has received to serve others, faithfully administering God's grace in its various forms.* (1 Peter 4:10)

Week 6: Where God Dwells

Leader's Weekly Journal
What has been the best thing you learned about yourself from this series on spiritual gifts? What difference would you like to see it make in your life? ...

Write out a prayer for the friends and family of group members.

Ask the Lord to begin the process of involving them more in the life of your small group. How could you really do that?

Ministry Time Questions, Week 1 - **Appendix A**

1. How does this idea of God's power at work in your life differ from what you've heard or thought about spiritual gifts in the past? How does it make you feel to know God wants to work powerfully through you?

2. Paul struggled to use his spiritual gifts. It's not easy to be available to be used by God powerfully. What are you struggling with that keeps you from being used by God more powerfully?

3. Spend a few minutes praying for each other. Ask for permission to lay your hands on the person's shoulder while you are praying. Share and pray for any personal needs as well (not prayer requests for friends, relatives, or co-workers).

--------------------------------- cut along this line ---------------------------------

1. How does this idea of God's power at work in your life differ from what you've heard or thought about spiritual gifts in the past? How does it make you feel to know God wants to work powerfully through you?

2. Paul struggled to use his spiritual gifts. It's not easy to be available to be used by God powerfully. What are you struggling with that keeps you from being used by God more powerfully?

3. Spend a few minutes praying for each other. Ask for permission to lay your hands on the person's shoulder while you are praying. Share and pray for any personal needs as well (not prayer requests for friends, relatives, or co-workers).

Appendix B1 - What do you think of me? Summary

What Spiritual Gifts do others see in me?

Make 3-5 copies of the facing page (Appendix B2). Now, give a copy to 3-5 to members of your small group who know you well and who are willing to be bluntly honest with you about who you are. Ask them to number the five gifts and related words that best describe you and return the assessment as soon as possible.

Person A	Person B	Person C	Person D	Person E	Spiritual Gift	TOTAL POINTS
					Pastor	
					Leader	
					Encourager	
					Evangelist	
					Teacher	
					Wisdom	
					Prophet	
					Faith	
					Knowledge	
					Helps	
					Administration	
					Service	
					Mercy	
					Giving	
					Discernment of Spirits	

Instructions:
As you transfer each person's numbers from their assessment sheet to this summary sheet, multiply the number for each spiritual gift using this point system:

1 = 10 points   2 = 8 points   3 = 6 points   4 = 4 points   5 = 2 points

(Example: Two people gave you a rating of 1 for "mercy" and the third gave you a rating of 2 for "mercy." Your total for Mercy would be 28 points)

Total up the points for each gift and write them in the column on the right (the highest number is your top spiritual gift). When you're done, list your top four spiritual gifts here:

1. _____   2. _____

3. _____   4. _____

What do you think of me? - Input From Others - **Appendix B2**

What do you think of me?

I am in a discovery process to learn about my spiritual gifts. Please take a few minutes to help me with your observations. What I most want to know is this: Where do you see the Holy Spirit working powerfully through me?

Instructions: Please select the top five areas you see in my life and ministry. Then, rate each one. In the left column, write a "1" by the most prominent, "2" by the next, and so on.

Rating (choose 5)	Areas of Supernatural Gifting You See In Me		Where have you seen this in my life?
	Pastor	Ability to care for and protect the long term spiritual needs of individuals or groups. People sensitivity.	
	Leader	Ability to provide overall vision for the Body of Christ and provide direction for others. Visionary.	
	Encourager	Ability to encourage, inspire, challenge, or rebuke others to action in positive, motivating ways.	
	Evangelist	Ability to share the Gospel in such a way that people respond, becoming followers of Jesus Christ.	
	Teacher	Ability to clearly and accurately communicate the truths of the Bible in such a way that people learn.	
	Wisdom	Ability to offer pertinent spiritual counsel in situations where guidance is needed. Applies godly insight.	
	Prophet	Ability to proclaim God's present and future truth in such a way that the hearers are moved to respond.	
	Faith	Ability to trust God with extraordinary confidence to work out His purposes in every situation.	
	Knowledge	Ability to receive and share revealed information not otherwise known; or clarify Biblical knowledge with unusually strong spiritual insight.	
	Helps	Ability to unselfishly meet the needs of others, freeing them to exercise their spiritual gifts.	
	Administration	Ability to provide organization for the goals of the body of Christ by designing and carrying out an efficient plan of action. Detail oriented.	
	Service	Ability to identify unmet needs, using whatever resources necessary to practically meet those needs.	
	Mercy	Ability to show great compassion for those who suffer physically, emotionally, or spiritually, and to assist them. Tenderness in action.	
	Giving	Ability to give freely, cheerfully, liberally, and sacrificially of one's money or possessions.	
	Discernment of Spirits	Ability to determine whether a certain action has its source in God, man, or Satan.	

Life of _____ Observed by _____

Appendix C - Gift Card

Where are you powerfully used by God?

Pastor	Knowledge
Leader	Helps
Encourager	Administration
Evangelist	Service
Teacher	Mercy
Wisdom	Giving
Prophet	Discernment
Faith	of Spirits

Where are you powerfully used by God?

Pastor	Knowledge
Leader	Helps
Encourager	Administration
Evangelist	Service
Teacher	Mercy
Wisdom	Giving
Prophet	Discernment
Faith	of Spirits

Listening to God Day By Day - **Appendix D**

As your read through one of this past week's Bible passages each day this week, what do you learn from the Lord that is a new understanding or an action you can do?

Read one passage per day, and start through them again after you have read each set of verses once. You will find God often speaks more clearly in multiple readings of the same passage, especially when you read them 3 to 4 days apart.

Monday   Scripture read:
Insight or Action:

Tuesday   Scripture read:
Insight or Action:

Wednesday Scripture read:
Insight or Action:

Thursday   Scripture read:
Insight or Action:

Friday   Scripture read:
Insight or Action:

Saturday   Scripture read:
Insight or Action:

Sunday   Scripture read:
Insight or Action:

Appendix E - Week 2 - Worship Reading

This week, the goal is to help your group experience worship by meditating on the Word of God. You will be reading one of the scriptures below *three* times. Prepare by reading both scriptures each day during your devotional time. Ask God to reveal himself powerfully through the scripture reading and worship experience you'll provide your group this week!

Deuteronomy 8:17,18:

"You may say to yourself, "My power and the strength of my hands have produced this wealth for me." But remember the LORD your God, for it is he who gives you the ability ..."

1 Chronicles 29:11-13:

"Yours, O LORD, is the greatness and the power and the glory and the majesty and the splendor, for everything in heaven and earth is yours.

Yours, O LORD, is the kingdom; you are exalted as head over all. Wealth and honor come from you; you are the ruler of all things.

In your hands are strength and power to exalt and give strength to all. Now, our God, we give you thanks, and praise your glorious name."

Week 3 - Welcome & Ministry Questions - **Appendix F**

Welcome Time Questions

1. Where did you live between the ages of 6 and 12?

2. What or where was a special place for you to go at that time in your life?

3. Who was the person who was always there for you when you needed him or her during those years?

Ministry Time Questions

Break up into triads to answer these next two questions and pray.

1. How aligned are your ministry/service/volunteer commitments with your spiritual gifts? Is there something you are not doing that you should be? Is there something you are doing you shouldn't be?

2. How might the amount of faith you currently possess influence your ability to have a "sober estimate" of yourself?

Take time now to pray aloud in your triad for yourself in the area of sober judgment, asking God to reveal his power and grace in your life. Be sure to pray in first person and "own" your prayers tonight!

> **The 65-35 Rule:**
> *"What if I'm involved in a ministry that doesn't suit my gifts?"*
>
> *One cannot sustain ministry for a long period of time in areas in which he or she is not gifted. That's why so many people burn out. Adjust your ministry activities so you are spending 65% of the time in your "sweet spot." In any family, there are chores to do, but try to keep the chores to less than 35% of your ministry effort. You will find this a sustainable ministry pace.*

Appendix G - Week 4 - Dream

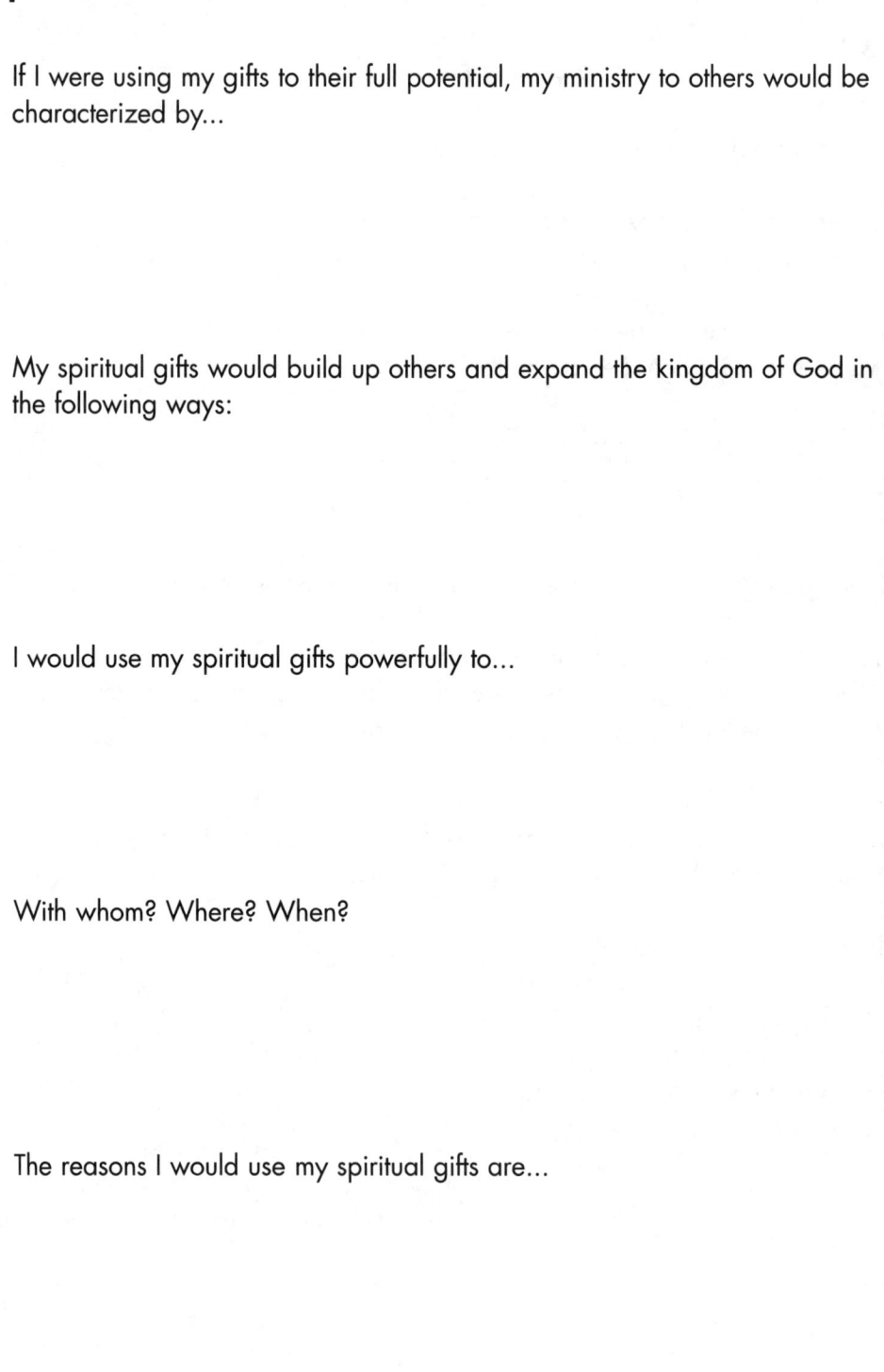

If I were using my gifts to their full potential, my ministry to others would be characterized by...

My spiritual gifts would build up others and expand the kingdom of God in the following ways:

I would use my spiritual gifts powerfully to...

With whom? Where? When?

The reasons I would use my spiritual gifts are...

Week 5 - Powerful in Words or Actions - **Appendix H**

1. What two, three, or four spiritual gifts were confirmed as your possible gifts? List them here in order of strength (strongest first, next strongest, etc.):

    a) _____

    b) _____

    c) _____

    d) _____

2. Compare your gift possibilities with the categories below – circle the gifts that are on your list.

    Powerful in Words
    Discernment of Spirits
    Exhortation
    Evangelism
    Leadership
    Pastoring
    Prophecy
    Teaching
    Wisdom/words of Wisdom
    Knowledge/words of Knowledge

    Powerful in Actions
    Administration
    Giving
    Helps
    Hospitality
    Mercy
    Service

Note: Faith turbo-charges the other gifts a person possesses, so it could fit in either category.

3. Do your potential spiritual gifts make you powerful in words, action, or a combination? Where do you see this to be true?

"If anyone speaks he/she should do it as if speaking the very words of God, If anyone serves, he [or she] should do it with the strength God provides, so that in all things God may be praised through Jesus Christ. To Him be the glory and the power forever and ever. Amen." (1 Peter 4:11)

Appendix I - Week 6 - Powerfully Moving Out In Practical Ways

1. What are some areas of ministry and service to one another in our group for which you may have spiritual gifts? (Here's a "starter" list – there are more possibilities!)
- ❏ Support – helps with basic group tasks week to week. (helps or service).
- ❏ Encourager – comes alongside individuals who want to grow spiritually. (exhortation or pastoring).
- ❏ Counsel – provide a listening ear to individuals or couples who are hurting. (pastoring, word of wisdom, or discernment of spirits).
- ❏ Facilitate application of the Word. (teaching, exhortation or prophet).
- ❏ Point person for evangelistic Bible studies with unchurched friends and family members of your small group. (evangelism or leadership).

2. What people might serve powerfully in the roles above, other than the people already fulfilling them? (Write their names below.)

3. What are some areas of ministry and service within or outside our church body where your gifts – or others in our group – could be utilized?
- ❏ Coffee host or hostess; greeter; usher. (hospitality)
- ❏ Hospital visitation. (mercy)
- ❏ Information Booth Administrator. (administration)
- ❏ "Adopt a grandparent or college student" participant; children's church teacher. (pastoring)
- ❏ Small group leader; small group coach. (leadership)
- ❏ Bible teacher, VBS class leader. (teaching, exhortation, wisdom)
- ❏ Missions team member; prayer team. (faith or intercession)

4. What are some areas of ministry and service in the community?
- ❏ One-to-one friendship evangelism. (evangelism or exhortation)
- ❏ Offer a parenting class quietly sharing biblical principles on discipline. (teaching)
- ❏ Join a civic group (ie Kiwanas) or neighborhood group to build friendships. (many gifts)
- ❏ Prison ministry. (mercy or exhortation)
- ❏ Coach little league or softball team and invite unbelieving friends. (pastoring, leadership)
- ❏ Start a cycling group or join a workout group with friends and be light and salt. (many gifts)
- ❏ Form a "builders club" that serves elderly or needy people by fixing up aging homes. (service, helps)

These are just a few samples of what might be possible.
There are scores of ways to use your gifts inside and outside the body of Christ!

Week 1 - Scripture Memory Verse - **Appendix J**

For it is by grace you have been saved, through faith—and this not from yourselves, it is the gift of God— not by works, so that no one can boast. For we are God's workmanship, created in Christ Jesus to do good works, which God prepared in advance for us to do. (Ephesians 2:8-10)

For it is by grace you have been saved, through faith—and this not from yourselves, it is the gift of God— not by works, so that no one can boast. For we are God's workmanship, created in Christ Jesus to do good works, which God prepared in advance for us to do. (Ephesians 2:8-10)

For it is by grace you have been saved, through faith—and this not from yourselves, it is the gift of God— not by works, so that no one can boast. For we are God's workmanship, created in Christ Jesus to do good works, which God prepared in advance for us to do. (Ephesians 2:8-10)

For it is by grace you have been saved, through faith—and this not from yourselves, it is the gift of God— not by works, so that no one can boast. For we are God's workmanship, created in Christ Jesus to do good works, which God prepared in advance for us to do. (Ephesians 2:8-10)

For it is by grace you have been saved, through faith—and this not from yourselves, it is the gift of God— not by works, so that no one can boast. For we are God's workmanship, created in Christ Jesus to do good works, which God prepared in advance for us to do. (Ephesians 2:8-10)

For it is by grace you have been saved, through faith—and this not from yourselves, it is the gift of God— not by works, so that no one can boast. For we are God's workmanship, created in Christ Jesus to do good works, which God prepared in advance for us to do. (Ephesians 2:8-10)

For it is by grace you have been saved, through faith—and this not from yourselves, it is the gift of God— not by works, so that no one can boast. For we are God's workmanship, created in Christ Jesus to do good works, which God prepared in advance for us to do. (Ephesians 2:8-10)

For it is by grace you have been saved, through faith—and this not from yourselves, it is the gift of God— not by works, so that no one can boast. For we are God's workmanship, created in Christ Jesus to do good works, which God prepared in advance for us to do. (Ephesians 2:8-10)

Appendix J - Week 2 - Scripture Memory Verse

The Spirit of the Lord came upon him, so that he became Israel's judge and went to war. (Judges 3:10)

The Spirit of the Lord came upon him, so that he became Israel's judge and went to war. (Judges 3:10)

The Spirit of the Lord came upon him, so that he became Israel's judge and went to war. (Judges 3:10)

The Spirit of the Lord came upon him, so that he became Israel's judge and went to war. (Judges 3:10)

The Spirit of the Lord came upon him, so that he became Israel's judge and went to war. (Judges 3:10)

The Spirit of the Lord came upon him, so that he became Israel's judge and went to war. (Judges 3:10)

The Spirit of the Lord came upon him, so that he became Israel's judge and went to war. (Judges 3:10)

The Spirit of the Lord came upon him, so that he became Israel's judge and went to war. (Judges 3:10)

The Spirit of the Lord came upon him, so that he became Israel's judge and went to war. (Judges 3:10)

The Spirit of the Lord came upon him, so that he became Israel's judge and went to war. (Judges 3:10)

The Spirit of the Lord came upon him, so that he became Israel's judge and went to war. (Judges 3:10)

The Spirit of the Lord came upon him, so that he became Israel's judge and went to war. (Judges 3:10)

The Spirit of the Lord came upon him, so that he became Israel's judge and went to war. (Judges 3:10)

Week 3 - Scripture Memory Verse - **Appendix J**

But you will receive power when the Holy Spirit has come upon you; and you will be my witnesses in Jerusalem, and in all Judea and Samaria, and to the ends of the earth. (Acts 1:8)

But you will receive power when the Holy Spirit has come upon you; and you will be my witnesses in Jerusalem, and in all Judea and Samaria, and to the ends of the earth. (Acts 1:8)

But you will receive power when the Holy Spirit has come upon you; and you will be my witnesses in Jerusalem, and in all Judea and Samaria, and to the ends of the earth. (Acts 1:8)

But you will receive power when the Holy Spirit has come upon you; and you will be my witnesses in Jerusalem, and in all Judea and Samaria, and to the ends of the earth. (Acts 1:8)

But you will receive power when the Holy Spirit has come upon you; and you will be my witnesses in Jerusalem, and in all Judea and Samaria, and to the ends of the earth. (Acts 1:8)

But you will receive power when the Holy Spirit has come upon you; and you will be my witnesses in Jerusalem, and in all Judea and Samaria, and to the ends of the earth. (Acts 1:8)

But you will receive power when the Holy Spirit has come upon you; and you will be my witnesses in Jerusalem, and in all Judea and Samaria, and to the ends of the earth. (Acts 1:8)

But you will receive power when the Holy Spirit has come upon you; and you will be my witnesses in Jerusalem, and in all Judea and Samaria, and to the ends of the earth. (Acts 1:8)

But you will receive power when the Holy Spirit has come upon you; and you will be my witnesses in Jerusalem, and in all Judea and Samaria, and to the ends of the earth. (Acts 1:8)

But you will receive power when the Holy Spirit has come upon you; and you will be my witnesses in Jerusalem, and in all Judea and Samaria, and to the ends of the earth. (Acts 1:8)

Appendix J - Week 4 - Scripture Memory Verse

For by the grace given me I say to each one of you: Do not think more highly of yourself than you ought, but rather think of yourself with sober judgment, in accordance with the measure of faith God has given you.   (Romans 12:3)

For by the grace given me I say to each one of you: Do not think more highly of yourself than you ought, but rather think of yourself with sober judgment, in accordance with the measure of faith God has given you.   (Romans 12:3)

For by the grace given me I say to each one of you: Do not think more highly of yourself than you ought, but rather think of yourself with sober judgment, in accordance with the measure of faith God has given you.   (Romans 12:3)

For by the grace given me I say to each one of you: Do not think more highly of yourself than you ought, but rather think of yourself with sober judgment, in accordance with the measure of faith God has given you.   (Romans 12:3)

For by the grace given me I say to each one of you: Do not think more highly of yourself than you ought, but rather think of yourself with sober judgment, in accordance with the measure of faith God has given you.   (Romans 12:3)

For by the grace given me I say to each one of you: Do not think more highly of yourself than you ought, but rather think of yourself with sober judgment, in accordance with the measure of faith God has given you.   (Romans 12:3)

For by the grace given me I say to each one of you: Do not think more highly of yourself than you ought, but rather think of yourself with sober judgment, in accordance with the measure of faith God has given you.   (Romans 12:3)

For by the grace given me I say to each one of you: Do not think more highly of yourself than you ought, but rather think of yourself with sober judgment, in accordance with the measure of faith God has given you.   (Romans 12:3)

For by the grace given me I say to each one of you: Do not think more highly of yourself than you ought, but rather think of yourself with sober judgment, in accordance with the measure of faith God has given you.   (Romans 12:3)

For by the grace given me I say to each one of you: Do not think more highly of yourself than you ought, but rather think of yourself with sober judgment, in accordance with the measure of faith God has given you.   (Romans 12:3)

Week 5 - Scripture Memory Verse - **Appendix J**

If anyone speaks he should do it as if speaking the very words of God, If anyone serves, he should do it with the strength God provides, so that in all things God may be praised through Jesus Christ. To Him be the glory and the power forever and ever. Amen. (1 Peter 4:11)

If anyone speaks he should do it as if speaking the very words of God, If anyone serves, he should do it with the strength God provides, so that in all things God may be praised through Jesus Christ. To Him be the glory and the power forever and ever. Amen. (1 Peter 4:11)

If anyone speaks he should do it as if speaking the very words of God, If anyone serves, he should do it with the strength God provides, so that in all things God may be praised through Jesus Christ. To Him be the glory and the power forever and ever. Amen. (1 Peter 4:11)

If anyone speaks he should do it as if speaking the very words of God, If anyone serves, he should do it with the strength God provides, so that in all things God may be praised through Jesus Christ. To Him be the glory and the power forever and ever. Amen. (1 Peter 4:11)

If anyone speaks he should do it as if speaking the very words of God, If anyone serves, he should do it with the strength God provides, so that in all things God may be praised through Jesus Christ. To Him be the glory and the power forever and ever. Amen. (1 Peter 4:11)

If anyone speaks he should do it as if speaking the very words of God, If anyone serves, he should do it with the strength God provides, so that in all things God may be praised through Jesus Christ. To Him be the glory and the power forever and ever. Amen. (1 Peter 4:11)

If anyone speaks he should do it as if speaking the very words of God, If anyone serves, he should do it with the strength God provides, so that in all things God may be praised through Jesus Christ. To Him be the glory and the power forever and ever. Amen. (1 Peter 4:11)

If anyone speaks he should do it as if speaking the very words of God, If anyone serves, he should do it with the strength God provides, so that in all things God may be praised through Jesus Christ. To Him be the glory and the power forever and ever. Amen. (1 Peter 4:11)

Appendix J - Week 6 - Scripture Memory Verse

Each one should use whatever gift he/she has received to serve others, faithfully administering God's grace in its various forms.   (1 Peter 4:10)

Each one should use whatever gift he/she has received to serve others, faithfully administering God's grace in its various forms.   (1 Peter 4:10)

Each one should use whatever gift he/she has received to serve others, faithfully administering God's grace in its various forms.   (1 Peter 4:10)

Each one should use whatever gift he/she has received to serve others, faithfully administering God's grace in its various forms.   (1 Peter 4:10)

Each one should use whatever gift he/she has received to serve others, faithfully administering God's grace in its various forms.   (1 Peter 4:10)

Each one should use whatever gift he/she has received to serve others faithfully administering God's grace in its various forms.   (1 Peter 4:10)

Each one should use whatever gift he/she has received to serve others faithfully administering God's grace in its various forms.   (1 Peter 4:10)

Each one should use whatever gift he/she has received to serve others faithfully administering God's grace in its various forms.   (1 Peter 4:10)

Each one should use whatever gift he/she has received to serve others faithfully administering God's grace in its various forms.   (1 Peter 4:10)

Each one should use whatever gift he/she has received to serve others faithfully administering God's grace in its various forms.   (1 Peter 4:10)

Each one should use whatever gift he/she has received to serve others faithfully administering God's grace in its various forms.   (1 Peter 4:10)

Each one should use whatever gift he/she has received to serve others faithfully administering God's grace in its various forms.   (1 Peter 4:10)

Each one should use whatever gift he/she has received to serve others faithfully administering God's grace in its various forms.   (1 Peter 4:10)

Each one should use whatever gift he/she has received to serve others faithfully administering God's grace in its various forms.   (1 Peter 4:10)